How to Launch Your
Teen's Career in Technology

A PARENT'S GUIDE

—— TO THE ——

T IN STEM
EDUCATION

SECOND EDITION

CHARLES EATON

Charles Eaton (2018).
How to Launch Your Teen's Career in Technology:
A Parent's Guide to the T in STEM Education 2nd Edition
Educational. Technology. Workforce Development.
1. Eaton, Charles

ISBN 978-164316889-0
LCCN 2017934416

Manufactured in the United States of America

Second Edition, Published April 2018

Dedicated To

Lindsay, Dylan, Mason and Shane
Thank you for bringing me the joy of being a parent
and letting me help you find your talents, skills
and inspirations.

Patti
For being my partner in this
fulfilling and frustrating journey
of life and parenthood.

People who succeed
in technology
are problem solvers.

TABLE OF CONTENTS

FOREWORD

Creating Inspiration

SOME OF MY EARLIEST MEMORIES are watching the last years of NASA's Apollo program. Sending astronauts to the moon and returning them safely to Earth had become routine by then, and every kid could watch each step of every mission on TV. Our nation's sense of pride and confidence in its technical prowess was infectious in those days. Technological innovations, such as the integrated circuit board, quickly (at least by early '70s standards) worked their way from the exclusive purview of space exploration into the everyday realm of commercial use.

My father was an engineer who eagerly shared his love of gadgetry with me by bringing home an array of electronics kits that were hitting the market. In a few years, I graduated from constructing cardboard rocket ships to building crystal radios, radio-controlled planes, gasoline-powered mini-cars and other pieces of technology available to any motivated youngster. By age 10, I had built a color television. My first computer arrived in 1979, a time long before every business had a mainframe in its backroom, a PC on every desktop and certainly a smart device in the palm of every employee's hand.

Yet, today, I'm an economist and analyst by education and training, not a technician like my dad. Oh, I followed in his footsteps all right, just not his occupation. He passed along more than a job title. He infused me with his passion for going beyond the technical, making inventions designed for exploring the heavens work for people here on the ground. My father inspired me to see technology not as the stuff of science fiction, but as the day-to-day science fact of helping people improve lives, businesses and the world around them.

Mom supported my deepening fascination, too, helping me appreciate the way a single piece of new tech can change the entire direction of an industry, or even society as a whole. Consider how Google redefined the use of the internet by defining the way we search it. Think of how Apple forever altered the course of the music business with the iPod or the development of cellular services with the iPhone. Contemplate how pioneers like Netflix rerouted how we rent movies or how upstarts like Amazon reshaped the way we buy everything.

If you look only at the surface, the technical level, you might believe these tectonic shifts in business and society were led by technologies, such as search engines, mobile devices or cloud services. No, these movements were led by technologists — naturally curious, creative individuals who think strategy first, love solving problems and enjoy working with humans more than hardware.

Technologists will lead the way in coming years, too. People, not computer code, will determine how virtual reality environments augment actual settings like construction sites, operating tables and classrooms. Human intellect, not artificial intelligence, will guide sophisticated robots — whether working on assembly lines or in cyberspace — as they manufacture goods, navigate highways or simply help make our workdays and weekends more productive and entertaining.

It's tempting to see educators and technical trainers as the answer to launching your teen's career in technology. But the secret isn't creating curriculum. It's creating inspiration. And not just in your children. In you as parents, too.

That's why Charles, my longtime friend and colleague, wrote this handbook. As a professional, his energy for developing our industry's workforce is unmatched, in my experience. As a person, his enthusiasm for helping people is unbounded, especially when the issue is giving disadvantaged or under-represented individuals a boost into the working world. And as a parent, his desire to not only instill young people with lasting self-confidence, but also supply them with practical tools for building self-reliance is unlimited.

No doubt my parents had supporters like Charles, as they lit my way into the future. With this book, I hope he inspires you to do the same.

— *Todd Thibodeaux*
President & Chief Executive Officer
CompTIA

Welcome to the T in STEM

TECHNOLOGY IS THE T IN "STEM," an acronym you've probably seen quite a bit as schools focus on science, technology, engineering and math classes. Technology fits nicely in the STEM collection, but it also stands on its own as a broad category of learning and skills that can appeal to a wide variety of student interests. Technology is not just a field for the brilliant and computer-obsessed; it's for anyone who likes to see how things work and wants to follow a problem to a logical conclusion.

At the same time, don't assume that because your kids seem better at using technology than you that they are automatically going to be able to grasp the bigger concepts needed for tech careers. While mobile phones are in the hands of most teens, there's a lot more to being ready for a tech career than being able to create a Snapchat story or post to Twitter.

I have four kids, two who are in elementary school and two who are their mid-20s at the time of this writing. My wife and I are on round two of being parents, with all the benefits of what we learned raising the older two. I know how hard it is to guide kids and help them figure out what they will like and what they will be good at doing. Too many of us default to the mantra of "get into college" with the hope that the light bulb will turn on for our kids before they graduate and move back home with us. But with the high costs of a four-year college education and the increasing number of alternative learning opportunities, such as online schools, community colleges and boot camp-style programs available at more reasonable prices, you should help your children find a path before they graduate high school. The good news is that there are more opportunities than ever for young people to explore tech careers, and this book lets you know where to start.

The objective of this book is to give parents of tweens and teens — from middle school through high school — an idea of what a technology career is really like, and how working in technology can be easier than you and your kids may think. We'll also bust some of the lingering myths about technology and show you an industry bursting with job opportunities perfect for eager students looking for careers that will dominate the economy in coming years.

— Charles Eaton, March 2018

Photo by Michelle Lange

The FrankenToyMobile tent at Chicago's annual South Side Mini Maker Faire offers projects that are interactive, kinetic and intelligent — a good way to introduce kids to the basics of technology.

Bust the Tech Myths
Technology Careers
May Not Be What You Imagine

TECHNOLOGY IS ABOUT LOGIC AND CREATIVITY rather than finding one right answer. It's a field in which people work together to solve individual, business and societal problems. It's also a career open to first-timers, offering fulfilling jobs that pay well right from the start.

People who succeed in the information technology industry break problems into pieces and solve them one at a time. It's not about being a genius or even learning how to write computer code. Technology is about being curious and trying to see the whole picture.

Technology is about solving problems instead of just living with them. People who work in technology are more likely to try again than to give up. And more importantly, they learn from failure.

Even if your child doesn't excel in math class, there are dozens of other positive personal attributes and interests that spell success in information technology. And they all add up to these facts:

 People who succeed in technology are problem solvers who care about other people and the overall quality of our lives.

 Successful technologists ask questions, challenge preconceptions and consider multiple conclusions before finding a solution.

 Anyone who understands technology and wants to use it for a larger purpose should consider a career in technology.

In this book, you'll learn some key traits of technology professionals and how to spot them in your child, such as:

• Does your child like to work with puzzles or Legos?

• Does your child take apart household gadgets, find glitches and dive in to fix them?

• Does your child help you fix the family computer when it's misbehaving?

Kids who like to take things apart to see how they work show great promise in the tech world because they develop into people who are driven to work on problems once others have admitted defeat.

Does your child care about big problems like world hunger or social injustice? Some of our best technologists are motivated to tackle those issues with technology solutions.

Put aside what you think you know about computers, software and mobile phones, and let us introduce you to the world of tech by busting some of the most common myths surrounding tech careers.

As a bonus, I will introduce you to a lot of people working in the tech industry — people who don't fit the typical stereotypes — who find satisfaction and growth in their technology roles.

These people didn't all come to the industry with a college degree, either. In the "Educational Pathways" chapter, you will learn that there are countless points of entry to the industry and dozens of ways to get involved right away.

Let's Bust the Myths

Despite all the benefits of working in the tech industry or a tech job, the word "technology" still alienates some people. We find that most people who are wary of technology careers have preconceived ideas about what it means. Some feel technology is too challenging, while others feel manipulating server racks would be so dull their eyes would glaze over. There's the view that pursuing a career in tech means you must be a recluse, sitting alone all day in a home or office tapping out obscure computer code. Some students believe that you must be a genius to understand and work with technology. It doesn't help that some of the most identifiable people in tech are clearly on another level intellectually — like Bill Gates and Mark Zuckerberg — or that pop culture depictions of tech jobs tend to fuel stereotypes of hackers or nerds. Let's face it: The image of the computer nerd is ingrained firmly in our society, and there are several studies that

Photo by Michelle Lange

Technology is a field that embraces imagination, creativity and having a little fun.

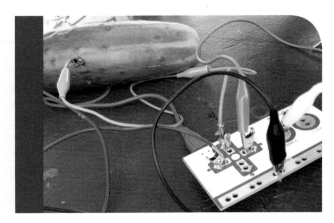

*Photo by
Michelle Lange*

A cucumber as a conductor? Technology is an imaginative world where kids learn new ways to solve problems.

show those stereotypes are still strong in the minds of younger people, especially young women. A University of Washington study found that media representations of the "stereotypical computer scientist" can be perceived as a "barrier to inclusion" by women.[1]

To dispel these misconceptions, I turned to experts such as Eric Berngen, who worked as a teacher and technology department chair at an early college STEM school, Sarah E. Goode High School in Chicago. Every year, he introduced the idea of technology to kids and parents who felt a little apprehensive about the subject.

"Technology is hard — that's a myth," said Berngen, going on to point out more misconceptions. "To learn technology, you have to be really good at math, or if you do it, you're a geek. I don't think that's true at all."

Technology is great for kids who like to find out how things work through tinkering and exploration. Technology is best learned when it's hands-on.

"Technology is a lot more about logic," Berngen said. "Do you understand the logic behind why things are behaving a certain way? Technologists break it down from a logical aspect."

Online videos feature dozens of free ways to explore different aspects of tech such as producing podcasts or working in graphic design. Free online programs and mobile apps help kids create interactive stories, games and animation. And advanced users can use the internet to learn more

1. Sapna Cheryan, Victoria C. Plaut, Caitlin Handron, Lauren Hudson, University of Washington. bit.ly/WashingtonEduPDF

complicated skills, such as building a computer, fixing hardware, writing code or setting up wireless networks.

"To be honest with you, there are so many blocks of free code available online, that if you're good at Googling and have a little logic, you can be a technologist," Berngen said.

As a parent, no one expects you to be a tech expert, but I want you to have enough information to start a conversation with your kids. Technology is always changing, but the core skills are pretty stable. You want to see your child succeed, to find a fulfilling, challenging career with room to grow. This book shows you what a tech career can offer, including an overview of the industry and the types of jobs available.

Still feeling apprehensive? Before I go any further, let's dispel some more myths about technology and tech careers.

MYTH: Technology is all about coding and math.

Resourcefulness and common sense are more important to future success in a technology career than excelling in math and science, and there still are more jobs in tech infrastructure — working with hardware, networks, servers and desktops — than in coding. In fact, data from Burning Glass Technologies shows that tech infrastructure positions make up 58 percent of the U.S. IT workforce.[2]

I know, if you've read the news headlines in the last few years, you'd think the only thing you should be doing is making sure your kid knows how to code. The tech entrepreneur success stories always seem to revolve around software and coding. The starting salaries for web and software developers are very high. Code.org has done a brilliant job of getting their Hour of Code into schools, and the Obama administration was a big fan of advancing coding and computer science. Those are all terrific developments that will help drive more young people into tech careers, but they could also discourage some kids for whom coding isn't easy, accessible or interesting. There's more to tech jobs than just coding. As more business and

2. Burning Glass Technologies data, Q4-2017

household devices connect to the internet and as more data is gathered and needs to be protected and understood, there will be plenty of jobs for technicians, network specialists, cybersecurity professionals and data analysts, as well as salespeople, marketing professionals and project managers.

The ability to listen, communicate and present new ideas are essential to succeed in technology. We refer to these as soft skills, but there's nothing soft about them. They are the foundation of success in technology and include skills such as conflict management, empathy and entrepreneurship.

While good grades are often important for opening up future opportunities, they don't tell the whole story about any student. Curiosity and motivation are more important than an impressive report card. The outlook for students in the academic middle — those who earn a respectable B or C in most classes and understand how to solve problems in the real world — is bright given the right training, encouragement and role models. Access to tech classes in school should not be dependent on how well one does in math. Every high school should showcase opportunities to learn and work with technology that are broader than computer science classes that are purely about computational thinking, or classes that simply teach students how to use Powerpoint and Word.

MYTH: To work in technology, you need a four-year college degree.

"In the world of technology, there's not a one-size-fits-all approach," Berngen said. "Technology is not a destination. It's about a journey."

There's more than one path to begin that journey because learning enough about technology to get a job can happen pretty quickly. According to the U.S. Census Bureau's 2015 American Community Survey, 59 percent of computer support specialists employed that year didn't have a bachelor's degree.[3]

A student can understand the underpinnings of technology and start troubleshooting problems or writing code after one introductory class, no

3. Burning Glass / 2015 ACS.
www.census.gov/programs-surveys/acs/

College By The Numbers

 **43 Million**
People Paying
Student Loans

 **$37,000**
Average
Student Loan Debt

+ $1.3 Trillion Owed

Tuition Costs Per Year

$ Two-Year $17,000

$$ Four-Year $24,000 In-State

$$$ Four-Year $39,000 Out-Of-State

$$$$ Private $48,000

 **58%**
Graduates Working
Full Time

 **$51k**
Average Salary of
College Graduates

Sources: College Board's *Trends in College Pricing 2015*, Student Loan Hero's *Student Debt Statistics*, National Association of Colleges and Employers

Photo from Chicago Tech Academy

Chicago Tech Academy invites tech mentors to speak frankly to students about working in technology.

matter at what age they start learning. In this book, I will share stories of people who learned about technology in high school and college, and others who started learning through online programs that are accessible to anyone, no matter where they live. The truth is that many people land a job in tech with just some basic training and a certification.

There's also the more traditional route of earning a computer science or information management degree, which isn't as narrow a road as many would expect. The development of intangible skills such as being flexible, adaptable and collaborative can begin in the classroom. These soft skills, which I referred to earlier, can help prepare young people for working in large organizations or small startup businesses. A structured program at the college level can familiarize students with workplace skills they will need on the job, such as functioning as part of a team and following the directions of a supervisor. Students also can begin to specialize in college, studying information systems, data analytics and similar courses. And there's a growing world of tech boot camps operated by private entities, such as General Assembly and Prime Digital Academy, that are helping students find their way into a software development or user design career in just a few months (even if they majored in English like me).

Technology moves quickly, and neither a four-year degree nor a certain set of certifications is a guarantee of success. Like any journey, the keys to pursuing a successful technology career are watching for bumps in the road without losing sight of the horizon, continually moving forward without wearing out, and, above all, being willing to adjust course while staying focused on the final goal. Because the one thing we can guarantee about technology is that it will evolve.

"In technology, you're constantly learning and everything is constantly changing," Berngen said. "Nothing stays the same."

MYTH: If it's not at Facebook or Google, it's not a technology job.

Technology has disrupted some big industries lately, such as hotels (Airbnb) and taxi service (Uber), and is the most important factor driving the global economy. But if you don't live in Silicon Valley, can you still work in technology? Of course. Despite their differences on the surface, every industry depends on IT. From small, family-run businesses — such as corner convenience stores, dry cleaners and lawn services — to big banks and insurance companies, there are IT careers in almost every organization around the globe. About 44 percent the tech jobs are in tech companies like Facebook and Google; the rest cut across all industries, according to CompTIA's 2018 IT Industry Outlook.

"Technology is not just at big companies," said Amy Kardel, who co-founded Clever Ducks, an information management company in rural California, where she says there are more cows than surfers.

Per the CompTIA *IT Industry Outlook 2018*, there are about 385,000 small information technology companies in the United States.[4]

"Technology is at little companies like ours, and there are companies like ours all over the country — all over the world," said Kardel.

There are thousands of jobs available at innovative companies, large and small, and plenty of places to work no matter where you live. As technology advances and telecommuting becomes more popular, the opportunities will multiply.

It's like I tell my youngest child, Shane. Shane wants to be an NBA player. Despite being named after Duke great and NBA champion Shane

---

4. CompTIA *IT Industry Outlook 2018*. www.comptia.org/insight-tools

Battier, the odds are against my little guy. He's not likely to be over 6 feet tall. His mom and I aren't elite athletes. And while he's got the most natural basketball skills of any of my kids, there are only about 500 current NBA players. I hope he has the drive, desire and luck to make it, but trust me, we'll have a backup plan. Part of that plan is to encourage him to think about all the different ways he might work in sports, especially with technology. He could be a technologist working on data analytics for an NBA coaching staff to help find the best defensive scheme for their players. He could be in broad-casting. Shane might even design the next app to track college basketball scores. We're a long way from having this be a substantive conversation, but I want to encourage his passion for basketball to be broader so it doesn't just fade away when he realizes he won't be a pro player. Think about how you could connect your child's passions to technology.

And speaking of passion, I've never liked the advice to "follow one's passion." That advice fails to acknowledge that we all have strengths and weaknesses and that enjoying your work can be as connected to doing something well as it is to the field of your occupation.

My early passions were technology and movies. I wanted to be a screen-writer when I was in college. Eventually, I realized that I didn't have anything that important to say or the discipline to write consistently enough to find a story that would make a good movie.

Instead, I focused on my strengths — problem solving and leadership — and found my calling in the nonprofit world. I am still connected to the tech industry through my work, and movies continue to be a nice hobby and distraction. There can be lots of ways to connect one's passions to meaningful and fulfilling work.

MYTH: A tech career means being stuck at a desk.

Technology connects us globally, and the industry is growing all over the world. There are plenty of tech jobs that don't require you to be chained to a desk.

Chicago-based artist, agent, writer and independent curator Jenny Lam uses her online platform to shine a spotlight on artists through unfiltered interviews. Her *Artists On The Lam* blog fosters art-based discussions and gives a behind-the-scenes view of the process of curating and installation.

Fashion designers use technology from concept and creation to delivery, thanks to innovative design programs and tracking chips.

An extension of her own creative outlets, Lam posts about the artists she represents, the exhibitions she curates and her art adventures around the globe. Art-related topics come up at local, national and international levels; her blog brings the world to her local readers, while making her surroundings more accessible to a global audience.

She's more than just a technology user, though, smartly using social media tools to position herself and her clients in the local press, and dipping into other sites as a guest blogger and featured Instagram photographer.

"I like how instant it all is and how you can be connected to people around the world all at once," Lam said.

MYTH: Money is the main benefit of a tech job.

It's true, technology jobs pay well, offering salaries significantly higher than the national average of all occupations. Unemployment in tech is low, and the future of tech professions looks good. According to the U.S. Bureau of Labor Statistics' *Occupational Outlook Handbook*, the availability of IT jobs is projected to grow by 13 percent during the current 10-year period

What Do Teens Want in a Career?

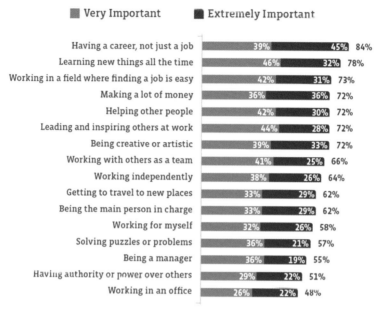

Source: Survey of Teen Views on Tech Careers, 2015 | CreatingITFutures.org

2016-2026.[5] However, what we've learned at Creating IT Futures (the nonprofit where I work) is that money doesn't drive everyone.

Like scientists, mathematicians and engineers, people working in technology like to solve problems. Driven by curiosity and empathy, they use big data to alleviate homelessness, for example, or get technology in the hands of people who lack economic opportunity.

Teens, too, want to help others and always be learning, according to what we found in Creating IT Futures' *Teen Views on Tech Careers* survey.[6] In the chart, you'll see that helping other people was near the top of the list of what teens want in a career.

5. U.S. Bureau of Labor Statistics Occupational Outlook Handbook. www.bls.gov/ooh/

6. Creating IT Futures *Teen Views on Tech Careers Survey, February 2015.*

Take Lakecia Gunter, who founded the Committee on Black Excellence at her high school. Lakecia received a computer at age 11, and later she used it to lobby teachers and other leaders at her school to find alternatives to suspending struggling students. Today, Lakecia is chief of staff to the CEO of Intel Corporation, one of the largest tech companies in the world.

Like many adults, teenagers want their work to affect more than a bank account. Working in a tech career has the promise of so much more than just earning a good salary.

MYTH: My kids won't listen to me.

Despite how many times the door gets slammed in your face, your teens trust you. There are times we've all felt that our words fall on deaf ears, but check this out: Creating IT Futures' *Teen Views on Tech Careers* study found that, in terms of advice on college and careers, teens rely on parents 2-to-1 over any other source, including teachers and friends. You're the one they will listen to, so it's important to educate yourself first.

Some key topics in this book will help in your conversations with your kids, but we are only scratching the surface. Everyone has preconceived notions about what a tech career means, but if you have some answers to your teen's questions, and can figure out where to find the other answers, your kids are likely to respect and listen to your advice.

MYTH: Tech jobs are going overseas.

Our digital world is expanding quickly, and it's creating technology jobs faster than companies can fill them. At any given point, more than half a million information technology job postings exist for open positions in the U.S., according to CompTIA analysis of labor insights data from Burning Glass Technologies.[7]

7. Burning Glass Technologies data, Q4-2017

Job Openings in Information Technology

Information technology jobs are still hot after a burst in openings, and as older tech pros retire, a new generation of skilled workers is needed to fill the gap.

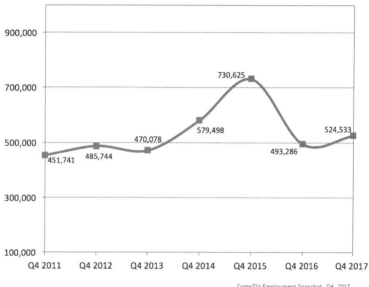

CompTIA Employment Snapshot, Q4, 2017

It's a staggering number of jobs that steadily grows. And despite what you might hear about globalization, plenty of tech jobs are being created in the U.S. or coming back to our shores. It's a field that shows no signs of slowing down.

How This Book Is Organized

Throughout the book, I hope to reframe the way you understand "tech careers." First, I will show you why the job market is hot, what kinds of jobs are popular and the high-paying salaries that come with even entry-level positions.

Then, I will share details that will help you to determine whether a tech career is right for your child. There's not a single mold for creating a technology professional, but there are traits that come up fairly often and patterns we find from studying people who are working in the industry. I will show you the skills needed to succeed in the industry, some programs and resources you can use and how to get your kids started right now.

Once you agree that a tech career may be an option for your child, you can read about the various paths that are available to her or him. A motivated do-it-yourselfer can take an online class or do some creative building at a makerspace (details in chapter 4). Students at many schools have access to a technology program, and there are a variety of after-school programs and clubs that focus on tech, but if your child's school isn't living up to your expectations, there are courses, boot camps and training programs where mentors will happily introduce an interested student to technology.

Finally, you will find out where the jobs are. There are technical and non-technical jobs in the information technology industry, as well as tech jobs in all other industries, including farming, finance and fashion. Today's world runs on technology, and there are opportunities everywhere.

Use this book as an introduction to tech careers, and share the message with your kids and their friends. Tell other parents what you've learned, too. "Each one, teach one," as the saying goes. The more we can work together and encourage our kids to explore all of tech's possibilities, the sooner we'll have a new generation of technologists innovating creative solutions for the world's challenges.

THE TAKEAWAY

Technology careers are about logic, curiosity, creativity and problem solving. They are accessible without a four-year college degree and there are hundreds of thousands of open jobs in information technology at any moment, all with the opportunity to earn a good living and advance through continual learning.

The Tech Job Market

More Than Half a Million Active Job Postings

MORE THAN HALF A MILLION JOB POSTINGS are waiting to be filled by curious and motivated people, and that's been the case for the last couple of years.[8] Most of those open jobs will be filled by people already working in another tech job. When that person leaves one job for another, there's another opening and so on and so forth. What does that mean for your kids as they prepare to enter the tech economy? Opportunity.

My job is to work with technology companies to solve problems for the entire industry. The cry I hear most often from those organizations is "We need more qualified people!" You may have read about the skills gap in tech — that there are jobs available, but not enough trained professionals to fill those positions. The reasons for the gap are complicated and could take the rest of this book to discuss. In short, it boils down to employers being dissatisfied with the candidates they are seeing.

8. Burning Glass Technologies data, Q4-2017

Photo by Michelle Lange

Hands-on projects make technology accessible and engaging for kids. Working with gear provided at a community robotics day, Noemi and Xochitl Chavez play with a Makey Makey hooked up to a conga, programmed to make a character on the monitor dance to the beat of the drum.

In a CompTIA survey, two-thirds of hiring managers expect filling job openings over the next two years will be challenging.[9] Reasons range from not finding candidates with the right experience, the right technical or soft skills or the appropriate salary expectations. In other words, there's opportunity for today's teens to build those skills now and be considered top candidates for open jobs in the future. On top of this skills gap, a whole generation of IT workers is about to retire, meaning there will be even more tech career options for today's teens.

A spark is all it takes to ignite a child's interest in technology, and compared to becoming a doctor or lawyer, it takes a fraction of the time — and a fraction of the financial investment — to learn the ropes. Exposing teenagers to the fundamental concepts of technology today opens them up to a variety of opportunities tomorrow.

Companies, governments and nonprofits increasingly rely on technology to solve countless problems. While technology does automate many processes, and can eliminate certain types of jobs, those who design, fix and integrate technology are well-positioned for the future. As of this writing, a mid-range annual salary in IT is $82,860 — a healthy wage that's more than twice the usual pay for all occupations.[10] Certainly, salary figures vary depending on factors such as location, job type and experience, but by any measure, tech jobs are high wage. In addition, many of these jobs are filled each year by people who don't have a four-year college degree or the debt that too often accompanies a diploma.

Each innovation in technology brings countless new job opportunities. Until the iPhone was launched, there was no market for developing mobile apps. Now look at that industry, with players big and small developing new tools for businesses and consumers every day. Careers in cybersecurity, app development, mobility and cloud technology are waiting for those motivated to pursue them. And these careers are available at organizations large and small, from coast to coast. As you'll learn throughout this book, there's a place in the tech industry for your child.

9. Employer Perceptions of IT Apprenticeships, February 2018.
https://www.comptia.org/resources/employer-perceptions-of-it-apprenticeships
10. CompTIA IT Employment Snapshot Q4 2017

Look Beyond Silicon Valley for Technology Jobs

If your city or state isn't listed, don't worry: There are nearly half a million jobs in information technology available across the U.S., with jobs in every state.

	Top States for Core IT Job Postings		Top MSAs for Core IT Job Postings
1.	California	1.	New York-Newark-Jersey City
2.	Texas	2.	Washington-Arlington-Alexandria
3.	New York	3.	San Francisco-Oakland-Hayward
4.	Virginia	4.	Los Angeles-Long Beach-Anaheim
5.	Illinois	5.	Chicago-Naperville-Elgin
6.	Florida	6.	San Jose-Sunnyvale-Santa Clara
7.	New Jersey	7.	Dallas-Fort Worth-Arlington
8.	Massachusetts	8.	Boston-Cambridge-Nashua
9.	Georgia	9.	Atlanta-Sandy Springs-Roswell
10.	Michigan	10.	Seattle-Tacoma-Bellevue

524,533 total US IT job postings in the fourth quarter of 2017
Source: Burning Glass Technologies Labor Insights, Q4 2017

Technology Offers High-Paying Jobs in a Variety of Fields

Technology touches nearly every part of business, government and non-profit efforts, and can be found in all industries. In a typical IT department, or a company that serves as tech support for other companies, those working in technology help people all day long. They maintain computers and mobile devices, outfit those devices with the right software and fix problems when they arise. Whether it's handled in person or remotely, desktop support and helpdesk positions are a popular entry-level role for someone who wants to begin a technology career.

Computer support is a common place to start a career in tech. With just a few classes or a certification, your son or daughter could get a job as a computer support specialist, solving computer software and hardware problems and helping others get the most from their technology. For an entry-level position, it comes with a good salary: The median is more than $52,160.[11]

11. U.S. Bureau of Labor Statistics, *2014-17 Occupational Outlook Handbook.*
bit.ly/USBLS-OOH2014-17

I'M A TECHNOLOGIST, TOO

Miranda Monahan
CEO
M-PowerTech

MIRANDA MONAHAN WAS NAMED one of the Top 50 Women-Led Business Leaders in Florida a few years ago — a long way from her start in IT as a receptionist.

In 2000, she was in college, answering the phone for a small IT dot-com company that sold desktops, laptops, printers and servers. The longer she worked there, the more she learned. One day, the sales director made her a deal: If someone called the office looking to buy a product or service, Monahan would be allowed to take on that customer as her own, earning the commission if she closed the sale. Little did this director know she would interview to work for Monahan 10 years later.

After some sales experience, Monahan updated her resume and got a job at Hewlett Packard, working there for six years, followed by ASI System Integration.

Monahan says her four years at ASI was a defining period of her career. "I was blessed with an amazing executive team who believed in me and constantly pushed me to excel. Because these accomplished executives believed in me, I began to believe in me."

"I would strongly encourage women to get their technical certifications and pick as many brains as you can," she says. "Women are great at sales in the IT industry, and if they have the technical knowledge behind them, there is no stopping them."

Setting up and fixing computer networks is a common step after the helpdesk, and it comes with a big bump in pay. A network and computer systems administrator works with the physical computer networks and typically earns more than $79,700 a year.[12]

Computer network architects design and build data communication networks, which range from a small connection between two offices to a multinational series of globally distributed communications systems. This is an area where growth is certainly expected, and where the usual salary is more than $101,210.[13]

According to the Bureau of Labor Statistics, web developers earn a good living as well, pulling in a salary of more than $66,130, on average.[14] Web developers design and create websites, and are responsible for how they look and perform. Software development is a little different, and technology pros with a talent for writing code can earn even more. Acting as the creative minds behind computer programs, some develop the applications that allow people to do specific tasks while others create the underlying systems that run devices and control networks. The typical salary for software developers is more than $102,280.[15]

> A mid-range annual salary in IT is $82,860 — more than twice the usual pay for all occupations.
>
> —U.S. Bureau of Labor Statistics

Some people are more about organization, and discovering ways to manipulate data. That's the role of a database administrator, who uses specialized software to store and organize things like financial information and shipping records. A database administrator earns $84,950 typically.[16]

12-16. U.S. Bureau of Labor Statistics, *2014-17 Occupational Outlook Handbook.* bit.ly/USBLS-OOH2014-17

Systems analysts are in demand, too. They study computer systems and procedures and then design technology solutions to help companies conduct business that's efficient and impactful. A computer systems analyst brings business and technology together by understanding the needs and limitations of both, and earns about $87,220 a year.[17]

Project management is another field in which jobs are available without a lot of technical knowledge. For example, someone needs to pull together all the pieces for a website launch, organizing the team and explaining things to both technical-minded folks and general business customers. Computer and information systems managers, often called information technology managers, or IT project managers, pull all these pieces together. They plan, coordinate and direct computer-related activities in an organization, plus set and implement technology goals for an organization. An experienced project manager can make about $100,000 per year.[18]

While we're swimming in affordable technology these days, we don't always know how to take the greatest advantage of the tools we have or how to protect the data we collect. That leaves room for hackers and information leaks, which every industry fears. That means one of the most in-demand tech specialties is in cybersecurity.

Cybersecurity is about defending against hackers and investigating how attacks took place. Information security analysts plan and carry out security measures to protect an organization's computer networks and systems. Their responsibilities are continually expanding as the number of cyberattacks increase. Information security analysts work for computer companies, consulting firms, government agencies and business and financial companies, where the typical annual salary is more than $92,600.[19]

More than Just Bro-Grammers

If you've read stories about the lack of racial and gender diversity in Silicon Valley tech companies, then you're aware that technology jobs are

17. U.S. Bureau of Labor Statistics, *2014-17 Occupational Outlook Handbook.* bit.ly/USBLS-OOH2014-17

18. Burning Glass Technologies

19. U.S. Bureau of Labor Statistics, *2014-17 Occupational Outlook Handbook.* bit.ly/USBLS-OOH2014-17

Melissa Hart
Owner & Operator
Bootstrap Communications

AFTER A CAREER in journalism, Melissa Hart honed her communication and marketing skills to start a business with a goal to "Do most good." As an independent consultant, she helps nonprofits and small businesses achieve greater impact through social media, fundraising, content, print and digital production, websites, design and email marketing.

Working for a rural development nonprofit in the Adirondack region of northern New York state turned her into a jack of all trades. "I was the de facto IT person for the 10-person office, setting up email accounts for interns and new staff, trouble-shooting website issues and other on-the-job situations as they came up," she said.

Now she's on her own and picking up clients all over New York State and across the country. "It's great to help clients make their ideas come to life," she said. Hart said a willingness to jump in and do what needs to be done has given her a career with a laid-back lifestyle — her preference to the city grind.

"Living in a rural place has its advantages," she said. "Your tech skills are in high demand."

often held by college-educated white and Asian men. That is starting to change, thanks to schools, companies and nonprofits all taking the lead to bring more women, people of color and young people from low-income backgrounds into the industry. My own organization, Creating IT Futures, has created on ramps to tech for young people and out-of-work adults that puts more diverse employees into tech occupations. There are dozens of similar groups focused on specific areas of the diversity challenge, such as Per Scholas, Black Girls Code, TechGirlz, CodeNow, TechCorps, Girls Who Code, Genesys Works, Year Up and The Stride Center.

A few years ago, Luz Chavez helped start Latin@ Techies to give back to her Pilsen community in Chicago and turn kids who were technology consumers into technology professionals.

"Latinos are the population most using cell phones and consuming technology, but only about 7 percent of us are working in technology," she said.

Through drop-in sessions, bilingual tech days and hackathons, the group brings together writers, coders and designers to explore technology-based solutions for community issues, like affordable housing. They also get families interested in technology and connect students with mentors who understand the industry and their culture.

Using their connections and background in technology, they partner with groups like Google and the National Association of Hispanic Journalists. Helping in the mission are her two co-founders: Lucio Villa, a hacker who started messing with computers growing up in Compton, California, and now works for the *San Francisco Chronicle*; and her brother, Jessie "Chuy" Chavez, a Google engineer who established computer science clubs at more than 100 schools in Chicago. "It's the first tech network in Chicago for Latino millennials," she said.

In San Francisco, the Women's Audio Mission (WAM) closes the diversity gap by matching the demographics of its students to its mentors. Students learn audio and media recording, production and sound design from established college-age mentors.

"We're at 82 percent girls of color, and we have to make sure there's a balance in our mentors, because that's what's going to make them connect," said WAM founder Terri Winston.

For its industry disruption, WAM won a Google RISE Award, which honors organizations that encourage girls and minorities to pursue careers in tech and computer science.

With all the promise for jobs and the potential to change the world in

Photo by Michelle Lange

Luz Chavez (right) co-founded Latin@ Techies to connect mentors who understand technology and Latino culture with inquisitive minds like Damian Alvarez.

Photo from WAM

Young women working with technology at the Women's Audio Mission in California are more interested in being sound engineers than pop stars.

a positive way, the tech industry must be representative of the people that are consuming its products. The old systems of hiring, educating and training aren't working well enough and new solutions must be developed and championed. That includes creating different types of opportunities for learning.

"If you have a room full of 18,000 men and throw a woman in there, it's a different experience. Or go to another country where you don't speak the language — it's hard to keep your confidence up," Winston said. "People need to get their confidence before they get thrown into an environment where they're a marginalized population."

Women Excel in Technology

I firmly believe that a diverse workplace generates unique and better ideas and getting more women involved in information technology is essential to growing the industry. Anecdotally and through research, we hear that young women avoid computer science classes because technology seems foreign or boring or that the stereotypes of a tech worker drive them away. As a male-dominated industry, it makes it hard for young women to envision themselves in technology roles. To reverse the gender gap, many groups are making technology careers more accessible to young women. And it appears to be working, as we are seeing gains for women in obtaining computing degrees and credentials.

"Technology offers tremendous opportunity for women," said Tracey Welson-Rossman, who founded TechGirlz, a Philadelphia nonprofit where middle school girls explore technology through free, hands-on workshops.

Women fill about 24 percent of core IT occupations, per the latest figures from the U.S. Bureau of Labor Statistics covering the last few years.[20] Growth in this segment has been sluggish, but the industry is focused on ways to entice more women to join.

"We're working to break the stereotype that a job in IT means you're closed up in a dark room writing code," said Cathy Alper, a founding member of CompTIA's Advancing Women in Technology (AWIT) Community.

"When you're looking for technology programs for your daughter, look for activities that make technology about problem solving and self-expression," said Winston, who has a terrific track record of bringing women into technology through WAM.

"The language of our crowd is that it's more about freedom of expression," she said. "You can express yourself and put it in a format that you can put on the internet."

At WAM, they use hands-on projects to engage students, like using Raspberry Pi computers to build synthesizers. "It takes literally an hour, but at the end they can say, 'I made this, and sound comes out!'" Winston said. "It has to be physical things and it has to be made meaningful."

Robotics, maker labs and web development classes give young women a chance to get hands-on with technology, especially if they're taught by enthusiastic and relatable women.

"The most important thing is that they're not just listening to someone tell them that it's interesting, they're actually getting to do it themselves," said Maria Klawe, a computer scientist, mathematician and president of Harvey Mudd College, a STEM-centric liberal arts college in Claremont, California.

If your daughter is considering computer courses, make sure she takes those that use a problem-solving approach to discussing theory and concepts, with lessons that let her practice what she's learned.

"Young women, as well as many young men, want to know what you

20. EMSI U.S. Bureau of Labor Statistics 2018 forecast

I'M A TECHNOLOGIST, TOO

Craig Brown
Technology Consultant, Big Data Expert
Techpreneur

SEEK OUT ORGANIZATIONS that support your computer interest and help develop your talents, recommends Craig Brown, the former national president of Black Data Processing Associates (BDPA). He's dedicated a good portion of his life preparing young people for STEM careers.

"That will help you find your path early on. You don't have to do it on your own," said Brown, whose dad worked with NASA's Space Shuttle program, impressing on him an interest in STEM education.

He found an interest in programming, turning mainframe data into reports that could be viewed on a PC. "It was so much fun," he said. "I got to create things and it was all brand new." That led him to full-time service as a Naval reservist, working primarily at the Pentagon.

"The military helped me because I got hands-on with big systems, large servers that nearly mimicked a mainframe."

Later he ran a nonprofit, BDPA, that teaches and mentors high school students in after school and weekend classes, gearing them toward a team web-design competition held each spring.

To get into information technology, he says get to know big data and open source software that can search unstructured databases, market your existing current computer skills, and get as much experience as you can. "There are jobs out there for people who have the skills," he said. "You just have to go through a training program."

can do with the things you learn in class, rather than just understand the concepts," Klawe said.

Find events for prospective students that include hands-on activities and show young women excelling in technology. "Young women can see fun, interesting things to do in areas they have not been exposed to in high school," said Klawe.

Look for female-focused programs sponsored by big names like Google and Facebook. "All the tech companies are just going crazy to find more women employees," Klawe said. "They are happy to help."

Once your daughter is excited about technology, help her retain that interest through group projects and research. "For women, in particular, feeling a part of the community is a very important experience," Klawe said. "Applying what you've learned so far to a research project is pretty exciting, too."

Lori Berry, director of strategic technology for Great America Financial Services, believes women are good at building relationships and tying things together at a higher level. She encourages young women to join the tech world by connecting new tools to their interests.

"We all should help them make that tie," Berry said. "If they're interested in veterinary medicine or fashion, help them understand that the more they know about technology in that area, the farther they are going to go in that profession."

In his unique position as vice president of sales and client development at F2OnSite, an IT services firm based in Dallas, Angelo Simao reads numerous customer satisfaction surveys and can tell by the results that women bring a lot of valuable skills to the industry. The company provides skilled people and technology resources for businesses across the country.

"In several studies we have conducted of our own business, communication scores and customer satisfaction ratings are higher across the board with female techs," said Simao. Women, he said, approach customers with more empathy. "They interact in a different way."

In the 20 years Simao has worked in staffing, he's seen a dramatic uptick in women working in information technology. That's thanks in part to groups like WAM and TechGirlz, which put technology in their hands.

"What's really interesting to me is how many girls connect with being an engineer," Winston said. "We'll ask, 'Who's going to be Beyoncé today?'

I'M A TECHNOLOGIST, TOO

Elliot Jobe
Senior User Experience Designer
BI Worldwide

A TRADITIONAL CLASSROOM isn't necessary to start learning technology skills. Find out what you're interested in, and learn as much as you can through online videos, tutorials and good old trial and error. That's what worked for Elliot Jobe, who got his start building websites for friends, learning as much as he could along the way.

Eventually, Jobe backed up his do-it-yourself skills with a degree in web design. After years of building sites, he now specializes in the consumer experience, which means putting himself in the shoes of those using his company's products.

"A lot of my job is speculative," he said. He's got to consider the types of phones and tablets people will be using in the next three years, for example, and plan for business expansion based on those speculations. It's the endless possibilities of the job that he loves.

"It's fun to predict future problems and try to solve them," Jobe said.

but instead they fight over being the engineer. They want to be in front of that huge console and a bajillion knobs and buttons and switches that they can be in control over."

Both groups give middle school girls a boost of confidence at an important time, according to Welson-Rossman. Around ninth grade, young women start self-selecting their futures and drop out of math and science classes. To keep them interested, TechGirlz presents technology as a creative outlet and a path toward the future.

"That's when the light bulbs start going off," Welson-Rossman said. "Technology is not just about coding or programming software. Technology is much, much broader than that."

THE TAKEAWAY

Technology jobs are dynamic and diverse, and open to women, minorities and anyone diligent enough to try until they succeed. Whether your teen is interested in creating new tools for the future or using big data to solve problems, technology offers countless career opportunities.

Photo by Michelle Lange

Exploration is the best way to decide if teenagers are into technology. Help them get their hands on some starter projects and see what happens.

Is a Tech Career Right for My Child?

Technology Lets You Think, Try, Fail and Succeed

ON THE FIRST DAY OF CLASS, former IT teacher Eric Berngen enjoyed the drama of telling his technology students, *"You are all going to fail."* His students attended a school specially designed for STEM fields, but many never had a computer class before. He used the theatrics to shake the nerves out of his students and help them dive in right away.

"When I'd say they were all going to fail, of course they all freaked out," he said. "Then I bring it back and say, 'We're *all* going to fail. That's part of the plan, and I'll fail right alongside you.'"

Berngen never worried about throwing his kids in the deep end because technology isn't anything to fear. There's more than one answer to a question like, "How would I customize a navigation bar?" Instead, his classes focused on trial, error and discovery.

"You'll get kids who buy in because they're not afraid of being wrong," he said. "A navigation bar is a navigation bar. It can be however you envision it."

To show them the fun side of technology, he and his students would program and fly drones after school, hack hardware and experiment with computer programming. They also used technology to invent problem solving tools — exactly what happens in the working world, too.

One student, tired of his phone battery always dying, worked up a phone case that holds onto the charger, too. Three young women in his class created video-based tutorials for students struggling with geometry. Another student built a remote server to control the environment of his favorite computer game, Minecraft.

"The best way to come up with innovation is to think of a problem you have and come up with a way to solve it," said Berngen. "Usually that's a formula for getting into actual innovation."

Identifying Technology Skills in Your Child

I work with technology pros all the time, and while every person I meet is unique, there are certain traits that line up with success in technology. Can you see these qualities in your child? Be honest with yourself — you want your child to succeed, but wishful thinking won't turn someone into a user experience (UX) designer.

Kids likely to succeed in technology often fall into at least one of these categories:

- **LOGICAL THINKERS** Kids who can follow a logical process do well in technology. Many projects involve lengthy, step-by-step instructions, and the industry needs people who are detail-oriented, focused and logical. My son Mason has been building the toughest Lego sets by himself since he was four. His ability to look at the instructions and put the right parts in the right place is extraordinary — far better than my wife or me. He finished a 4,000-piece Disney castle in two days. Those are skills he definitely can use on the job someday.

- **INNOVATORS** Does your son or daughter see a problem and figure out a way to solve it? It might be a new process they invent or a

Photo from Vocademy

Technology comes alive when hands-on experience meets design and making. It's a great entry into the world of technology.

physical device they build or something really cool made from littleBits kits. No matter the solution, your child might love the various ways that technology can be deployed to do something new.

TINKERERS If you have a kid who toys around with things a lot, that's another good sign you've got a future technology pro on your hands. Kids who like to take things apart (and put them back together) to see how they work have a lot in common with people I know in the technology industry.

COMMUNICATORS Technology professionals spend a lot of time working with people who don't understand computers, so communication skills and the ability to explain things in simple terms are critical. So is empathy, which lets you see a problem from the other person's point of view.

PROJECT MANAGERS Understanding a wide range of perspectives is helpful, too. Students who know how to coordinate a big group or get a big project done by breaking it down into smaller parts surely will succeed in information technology.

CREATIVES Curiosity and creativity will take your child a long way in this industry. Technology pros create and identify products, services and solutions that work for both a business and its customers.

FLEXIBLE LEARNERS The ability to change gears and try out-of-the-box ideas is essential in an industry that changes quickly. So is keeping up with new ideas and learning the latest technologies and computing languages. Companies want to hire people who are flexible to their ever-changing technology needs.

Get Started

I encourage you to keep reading this book to learn more about the industry and see great examples of happy, productive people working in technology. From there, exploration is the best way to decide if technology suits your child. To get started right away, we offer some resources for exploring information technology, and all the opportunities our industry offers.

1) Better Understand Tech Careers

Technology provides great pay and a flexible lifestyle, and jobs are in high demand. Start looking around and you'll see technology pop up in places you never expected. Tell your kids they can find work in the information technology industry, or work with computers in finance, entertainment, education or healthcare.

Photo by Michelle Lange

A Raspberry Pi is a tiny computer used to introduce kids to technology.

What's Up with IT? is a dynamic infographic that walks you through what it takes to find a career in technology.

certification.comptia.org/whatsupwithIT

Get into IT is a colorful brochure by CompTIA that summarizes many of the points already covered in this book.

certification.comptia.org/why-certify/students

Cyberseek provides detailed, actionable data about supply and demand in the cybersecurity job market.

cyberseek.org

LifeJourney allows students to test drive future STEM careers and learn directly from top industry professionals.

lifejourney.us

Test Drive an IT Career with this video series by CompTIA and Creating IT Futures. The videos introduce students to real IT workers and help them answer the question, "Is an information technology career the right fit for you?"

comptia.org/testdrive

2) Get Hands-On

Before your teen dives too deep into information technology, have her try it on for size. Find a project your teen wants to do and start with some trial and error. If you can, get your hands on some introductory tools that make technology fun and creative, such as the Raspberry Pi and the programming language called Scratch.

A Raspberry Pi is a palm-sized, single-board computer developed to promote basic computer science education skills for students.

raspberrypi.org

littleBits makes a platform of easy-to-use electronic building blocks empowering everyone to create inventions, large and small.

littlebits.cc

BOSEbuild believes kids are creative, imaginative, curious creatures who deserve tools that inspire their curiosity and spark their instinct for exploration.

build.bose.com

Scratch is a free program that lets you create interactive stories, games, and animations — and share them with others in the online community.

scratch.mit.edu

Code.org believes every student in every school should have the opportunity to learn computer science, just like biology, chemistry or algebra.

code.org

FUSE is an interest-driven learning experience developed by researchers and educators in the School of Education and Social Policy at Northwestern University.

fusestudio.net

TechGirlz is a nonprofit organization dedicated to reducing the gender gap in technology occupations by offering educational hands-on workshops and summer camps.

techgirlz.org

6 Signs You Have a Quality High School Tech Program

1 A teacher who is passionate about teaching technology and consistently puts in outside time to work with students.

2 A hands-on classroom working on activities students can relate to.

3 Encouragement to earn a certification or learn more through tutoring sessions and peer-to-peer coaching.

4 Good communication about expectations for the classes and opportunities in technology.

5 A holistic culture of computer learning through extracurricular clubs and technology competitions.

6 Formal ways to connect students to workplace learning and earning opportunities, including internships and job shadow days.

The New York Academy of Sciences (NYAS) is an independent, nonprofit organization that, since 1817, has been driving innovative solutions to society's challenges by advancing scientific research, education, and policy. NYAS, Creating IT Futures and CompTIA work together on a series of mentoring programs for young people.

nyas.org

 Technology Student Association (TSA) holds 60+ STEM competitions at their national conference each year, where students compete in debates about technological advances and their impact, learn how to code and design video games. The group has more than 2,000 school chapters in the U.S.

tsaweb.org

3) Explore What's in Your Area

I often hear that when parents see their kids interacting with technology, that's when the light bulb goes off in their mind. Find a youth group in your area that lets kids explore technology through creativity and you'll see their eyes light up at the possibilities.

Use a basic Google search or one of the directories we've listed here to see what opportunities are in your area. Once you start looking around, you'll realize technology learning opportunities are everywhere.

 The Connectory makes the connections to STEM learning opportunities that inspire young people to explore, discover, and create.

theconnectory.org

 STEM-Works is a resource for teachers, mentors, parents, STEM professionals, volunteers, and everyone passionate about getting children eager to learn about science, technology, engineering and math.

stem-works.com

Technology Councils of North America is a collection of state and regional tech councils, many of which sponsor programs to inspire youth toward STEM careers. You can find your regional tech council on this site.

tecna.org/map

4) Take a Class, Get Certified or Compete

If your child finds that they have a definite interest in information technology, they can start considering education and certifications that can help them to continue the journey. Resist the temptation to handle this work for your child. The best way for kids to discover their potential in technology is to take action themselves.

Certifications show focus and commitment to potential employers. A student who takes the time to learn the material and tests well enough to earn a certification will be ahead of other candidates pursuing the same job opportunities. In a study by CompTIA, 43 percent of employers said they expect the need for IT certifications for new hires will grow in the next two years. [21]

A technology certification is an increasingly compelling document when you're applying for a job. However, be aware that in some tech specialties such as web and software development, there are few, if any, certifications that employers look for. Instead, employers want to see a portfolio of projects that show one's skills.

The CompTIA IT Certification Roadmap makes navigating the world of certifications easier. Follow the map to understand all the jobs available, and the certifications that will help get you there. Download the PDF and print it out.

comptia.org/roadmap

21. Employer Perceptions of IT Apprenticeships, February 2018.
https://www.comptia.org/resources/employer-perceptions-of-it-apprenticeships

Skillsboost helps students, parents and educators discover how to launch and develop a career in information technology through certifications.

skillsboost.comptia.org

 Codecademy is one of several websites where one can learn to code for free.

codecademy.com

 Cyberpatriot is a program from the Air Force Association that includes a national competition in which teams compete to manage a network for a small company and protect it from outside attacks.

uscyberpatriot.org

THE TAKEAWAY

People who succeed in technology ask questions, challenge preconceptions and consider multiple conclusions before finding a solution. Anyone who understands technology and uses it for a larger purpose should consider a career in technology.

Educational Pathways
Mentors Make All the Difference

AS A TEENAGER, Christopher Brito's life was stuck in neutral. He didn't care about school, had few plans for the future and was enrolled in a stop-gap program that does its best to keep dropouts in school until gradua-tion. There, at the Latin American Youth Center Career Academy in Wash-ington, D.C., he met a mentor who introduced him to technology.

Information technology teacher Abner Soto taught Brito about com-puters. Brito learned how to troubleshoot technology problems, mount servers and manage networks. In just one year, he learned the basics of technology, engaged in a hands-on internship and earned certifications that helped him land his first career-based job. Now, he's a certified com-puter technician working in Texas, helping support his family and happy to have a career in technology.

"Opportunities like this don't come every day, and you've got to take them when they come," said Brito.

Photo by Abner Soto

Chris Brito became a technologist after one year of classes and mentoring. "That program changed my mentality a lot," he said.

Learning about technology made him more focused in school, more interested in computers and more engaged in current events. "I started reading. I started looking stuff up on the internet. I started watching the news. I couldn't stop," he said. "I still can't stop."

At Creating IT Futures, we hear success stories like Brito's all the time: "I didn't know what I wanted, but then I found technology and realized I could have a career."

Technology gives students a new outlook on their careers and hope for the future. Brito's story is also a great example of the kind of person we want to join the industry. He's creative, curious and willing to learn. Technology can be challenging, but it's easy to dig in and get started.

No matter where you live, there are probably technology programs available. High school programs expose kids to technology and help them feel more comfortable with it, and community college programs often offer dual credit for students (both high school and college credit), so they can double dip on their efforts.

Two- and four-year colleges are a traditional path to technology careers, and many offer internships and certifications so that students can go straight from the classroom into jobs. Online schools and bootcamp-style accelerated learning programs are also entry points to technology careers. And makerspaces give students a chance to get involved with technology while having a lot of fun.

I'M A TECHNOLOGIST, TOO

Andrea Rios McMillian
Workforce Strategy & Innovation Manager
Creating IT Futures

ANDREA RIOS-MCMILLIAN WAS THE FIRST in her family to graduate from college. Though, when she was younger she figured her job options were limited to what she saw her Mexican family members doing: contracting, factory jobs and cutting hair.

"When we would talk about our futures in class, my friends would say, 'I want to change the world,' but for me I thought, 'I'm going to be a barber like my mom.' That's all I knew."

During a class lesson on the judicial system, she got a chance to participate in a mock trial as a lawyer, which opened her eyes to new career possibilities. "I remember the work being fascinating, and it was the first time as a Hispanic woman and a minority in a predominantly white school that I thought, 'I *can* do this — I *can* change the world, too," she said.

She credits the start of her career in technology to her early days working at Best Buy. "My manager pushed me into the technology side of the business and gave me exposure to other women working in senior leadership positions. Seeing them excel in technology gave me the confidence to do the same. Soon I was leading our most profitable segments including computing, tablets, mobile phones and tech support services."

Today, Rios-McMillian helps parents and businesses get children excited about technology. "It's so important to get kids connected not necessarily to career planning, but to open their eyes to what they can do," she said.

High School Students Respond to Hands-On Learning

Seth Reichelson, who teaches Advanced Placement (AP) Computer Science at Lake Brantley High School near Orlando, Florida, favors hands-on learning over the textbook exercises students encounter in math classes. He believes emphasizing the mathematical underpinnings of computer science overcomplicates the subject.

"One of my problems is this predetermined stereotype of what computer science is," Reichelson explained. "It's not calculus. You have to know 40 terms maybe. And after the first few weeks, students are like, 'I can do this.'"

A big reason his students feel so empowered to learn is Reichelson keeps lessons simple and focused on outcomes rather than processes.

For example, the first assignment his class tackles is "Bunny Bears Having a Party Using Turtles." A more technical name might be: "Instantiating Objects and Using Methods in Java," but "Why would I make the first assignment in the class really intimidating?" he said.

At schools across the country, students dive into technology thanks to teachers like Reichelson and Kevin Kelly. Kelly cares less about how much the student knows and more about their interest in technology.

Photo by Abner Soto

Jose Morales learned how to help people with technology issues in his studies at the Latin American Youth Center Career Academy.

"They don't have to know anything about computers, but they have to have the passion to learn more than just what's given to them on a daily lesson," said Kelly, who teaches technology at the McKenzie Center for Innovation and Technology in Indianapolis, Indiana.

Once they have a handle on basic troubleshooting and hardware repair, his students take their classroom knowledge into the real world, lending a hand at the nearby Metropolitan School District of Lawrence Township. By repairing and resetting computers for incoming students, kids get a sense of what an entry-level technology job is like.

"It's a great opportunity," Kelly said. "We do a lot of learning and hands-on in the lab, but actually getting out and doing it on the job is a big difference."

At the Latin American Youth Center Career Academy, students dive into technology on day one. "We basically show them, 'This is the motherboard, this is the CPU and this is the software on which you're going to build a computer,'" said Soto, who mentors students like Brito every year.

After a week of putting parts together and taking them apart in class — sometimes under rigorous time trials — the students have taken an important step toward a career in information technology. "They're like, 'Wow, in just one week I did that!' They're very excited," he said.

It's the same story in the suburbs of Chicago, where juniors and seniors at Leyden High School get a taste for the working world in an elective class that functions just like an IT helpdesk.

Leyden students share the workload of answering the phone and responding to emails, writing and assigning tickets and troubleshooting problems, everything from fixing loose cords to changing out motherboards. They also help teachers set up labs and work on independent pathways to complement their studies, like learning a programming language or studying for a certification such as CompTIA A+.

"Sometimes there are tougher tickets, where a student will have to get up in front of another class, get on a ladder and fix a projector in front of people," said Tony Pecucci, a technology teacher who helped launch the internship with the backing of the school district and a technology advisory board. "Those moments can be good for building self-esteem in front of their peers."

Now replicated in dozens of schools, the class gives students in the economically diverse and heavily Hispanic suburban school a chance to be the expert, and get experience in ticket-writing, technical writing and general customer service.

"In some of our experiences, our students are beating out college graduates for jobs," Pecucci said. "The college students don't have real-world experience with ticketing or troubleshooting. Our students can write a technical ticket. They know how to work with people and how to work with adults and other students. They have experience answering the phone in our room and handling a lot of the incoming traffic."

In El Paso, Texas, members of the Aztec Network Technology Society (ANTS) learn technology skills in school and spend Saturdays fixing broken computers for local groups and nonprofits, like the H.O.P.E. Institute for homeless female veterans, operated by retired Lt. Col. Hope Jackson.

This kind of service work not only helps others, but gives the students great hands-on experience, according to David "King FOG" Caldwell, a technology teacher at El Dorado High School in El Paso. Caldwell is an imaginative teacher who uses symbolism from medieval times and martial arts to get students interested in technology. The program also boasts a 60-to-40 girls-to-boys ratio.

"I really think it's a special program," said graduate Jacob Rey. "We got to troubleshoot computers. We got to use tools that we never heard of. We'd fix computers that were old and we had to make them run again. This is where the money is at. This is where we are going to get jobs."

The school's second technology club is called the Fellowship of Geeks (FOG), which makes students feel included with a secret hand signal and members-only promotional ceremonies. FOG is more of a social club, where students encourage each other as they prepare for certification exams.

The FOG's aura of secrecy gives all its members a "beautiful sense of belonging," said El Dorado's former Principal Nora Paugh. "They have taken something that probably they have been teased about in the past and elevated it to such a prestigious organization."

These programs are essential to cities and towns that struggle to provide good jobs for graduates. "Businesses are trying to look to the future, and they know a lot of young people leave El Paso," said Derrick Brown, former assistant principal at El Dorado.

Photo by Eric Larson

El Dorado High School technology teacher David Caldwell connects with students by letting them be silly, creative and collaborative.

Claudia Casas' daughter Bianca enrolled in the technology program. She's happy the program encourages young women to succeed in technology, and imagines the experience her daughter and her friends had will translate to jobs in the future. "They could be working after high school, while they are in college, or even working for big companies," Casas said.

I'M A TECHNOLOGIST, TOO

Matthew Pineiro
Senior Analyst IT Infrastructure,
Colony NorthStar Inc.

SYSTEMS ENGINEER MATTHEW PINEIRO relates to the intimidation one might feel looking at a giant data center server rack, but he also knows that once you break things down to smaller parts, even complex solutions start making sense.

"Everything builds upon another thing," said Pineiro. "I think most people would be pretty surprised with their ability to work in this field."

Pineiro designs technology solutions for customers, and then puts them into action. Because he's got to sell customers on his ideas, his soft skills and ability to connect with people come into play just as often as his ability to do math.

"You don't have to be great at math," he said. "If you can add and subtract and do basic multiplication and division, you're halfway there."

It's coupling soft skills with technical training that will keep you moving up the ladder.

"Before you know it, you're going to look back and say, 'I never thought I'd get to this point, I never thought I'd understand these things I'm doing, but now it's just second nature.'"

El Dorado and Leyden offer students the chance to get certified in IT skills. Certifications from CompTIA offer a vendor-neutral education, while certifications from well-known tech vendors such as Cisco and Microsoft are tailored with a product-specific approach. CompTIA has thousands of academic partners — places where budding technology professionals can study for the certification and take the test, too.

"Schools like El Dorado and Leyden are the connective tissue between the altruistic side — making IT skills more available to the general public — and our mission to prepare high school students for employment, giving them an avenue to becoming an IT professional," said Richard Tung, Vice President, Product Management and Marketing at CompTIA, who works regularly with the organization's academic partners.

"We have these partnerships so we can extend our reach and offer certification training and testing in as many places as we can," Tung said.

Programs that couple in-class learning with on-the-job experience give students a leg up in the job market, said Walt Jaqua, who teaches technology classes in South Bend, Indiana. "There are employers looking to hire entry-level students directly from the program," Jaqua said.

His students get real-world training while they study and test for IT certifications that count toward college credit and qualify them for jobs after graduation.

"I spend a lot of time one-on-one with students just discussing their background, what they like about technology and where they feel like they want to go," Jaqua said. He exposes students to different career paths and tries to match their aptitude and work ethic with the right jobs. "As they progress through the program, I want to tailor everything they do to meet their goals."

Employers are happy to hire students right out of school, he said, because they can be trained in the company's style.

Kelly's graduates can be found in companies all over Indianapolis, including Simon Property Group, Bell Techlogix, Computer Express, Fry's Electronics and Best Buy's Geek Squad.

"There are still more IT jobs than there are people to fill them," said Jaqua. "It's an in-demand field."

I'M A TECHNOLOGIST, TOO

Stephanie Hasz
Comedian, Festival Producer and
Software Engineer, NowPow

COMEDIAN STEPHANIE HASZ'S unique voice has earned her a place in Chicago's comedy scene, and her web skills and ability to put plans into action helped launch an independent comedy festival that draws emerging stand-up talent from around the country.

As one of the founders of The Comedy Exposition, Hasz handled all technical activities for the event, plus the logistics and financial planning.

She relied on social media and internet connections to add fans and attract fresh talent to the lineup. Behind the scenes, she put her tech skills to work, ensuring the festival planning ran smoothly.

Data management was a bit of a snag during the first year of the expo, as the organizers found themselves caught in a web of emails and shared documents.

Hasz put her technical skills to work and built a custom content management system so they could accept submissions and share information directly through the website, making the event easier to manage — and more fun to experience.

"Technology helped me create a great project with my friends, which turned into a great experience for our audiences," she said.

College Programs Let Students Double Dip on Their Efforts

There are plenty of online and college courses for your teenager to try if the local high school doesn't offer a technology program. Often, those classes are offered as "dual credits," meaning students earn high school and college credit for taking the same class.

That's the case with the Computer and Internetworking Technician program at the College of DuPage in Glen Ellyn, Illinois, which adapts its programs to emerging technology like computer forensics, cloud computing, virtualization and mobile applications.

"The classes are very focused toward what people are doing in the real world," said John Kronenburger, visiting professor of electronics and electromechanical engineering technology at College of DuPage. "It's a nice entry and exit point for people looking for specific specialty needs."

Students in the program get hands-on experience interning at local businesses like the Argonne National Laboratory and Chicago Computers. Many of the secondary education programs include mentoring, too, because helping students feel connected to the learning process makes them more likely to succeed.

Mentorship plays a key role at Western Governors University, an online school with a robust technology program. Adrian Genesir helps students learn about technology and coaches them through certification exams to help back up their skills. "It's just amazing the amount of students we have helped achieve a degree," he said.

Even though his students are geographically far away, he feels their enthusiasm and celebrates when they pass a certification exam. For his students, certifications help them land jobs, earn bonuses and get promoted even in the face of an uncertain economic landscape.

"When they pass a certification, it's like a big party," he said.

At programs like Tidewater Community College in Chesapeake, Virginia, students can get into technology through two-year associate degree programs, one-year certificate programs, and through career and workforce development programs. Workforce development courses are offered on campus and online.

Lonnie Barnes attended classes there and realized technology offered him a lot more than what he was doing previously: painting ships and submarines at a Newport News shipyard. Thanks to Tidewater, he realized his dream of starting his own company from the ground up, based in technology security.

"Honest to God, I wouldn't have come to that conclusion without coming to Tidewater," he said. "They have the tools, the background and the people to make it happen."

A natural born tinkerer, he took apart his grandparents' television set when he was 10 because he wanted to see how it worked. It took a long time for him to connect his love for tinkering with a technology career, and as a teacher at Tidewater, he helps students make that connection faster than he did.

"My main goal with all my classes is getting people certified," Barnes said, and he means it. "I tell my students in the first week of each course, 'It's going to be hard sometimes, but I promise that if you do the work, you will get certified.'"

As jobs in networking and security open up, specialized technology degrees are starting to appear. The State University of New York at Plattsburgh, for example, recently launched a computer security major for its 6,000 students.

The four-year liberal arts college, located just north of the Adirondack Mountains, is one of the only SUNY schools offering a security-specific degree.

"Computers are everywhere and in everything," said Dr. Delbert Hart, professor of computer science, announcing the program in the school's alumni magazine. "There is a growing demand for specialization in computer security."[22]

Several schools in the University of Maryland system are offering cybersecurity degrees as well to take advantage of their proximity to the growing number of cybersecurity jobs in the Washington, D.C. region.

---

22. Dr. Delbert Hart, Professor, Computer Science, The State University of New York (SUNY) at Plattsburgh. bit.ly/PlattsburghMagSummer2015

I'M A TECHNOLOGIST, TOO

Shannon Branch
Support Engineer
Guidance Software Inc.

BORN TO DRUG-ADDICTED PARENTS in New York, Shannon Branch spent her first seven years in North Carolina foster care before returning to the city, where she struggled through high school. She graduated and tried college, but didn't have a strategy to deal with the intense workload.

Through a friend she learned about Per Scholas, which offers technology training to low-income people and helps them find jobs. "They offered technology — the future," Branch said. "I saw this as a chance to finally have my own future, too."

She took a challenging all-women's class, and her persistence paid off. She now has role models and a new perspective about technology.

"One of the best things Per Scholas did was invite four women who work in the field to come and talk to my class," Branch said. "Three of them were African American and one was Hispanic, and they told us their trials and tribulations."

She was inspired by them, working in an industry where just 3 percent of the professionals are minority women. "They're making change," she said, "and they gave us courage and confidence, because they're the proof that we can do it, too!"

For Driven Teens, Try Bootcamps and Training Programs

Outside of the classroom, there are hundreds of boot camps and training programs that can be taken online and in-person, or as a hybrid of the two. With an internet connection and some self-determination, your child can start learning about technology from anywhere. Codecademy, Treehouse, Coursera and others offer popular tools for learning to code online. After graduating high school, your child might consider a coding bootcamp, and websites such as Coursereport.com list programs, offer student reviews and even highlight scholarships to help a student get started. For the self-motivated teenager, a career in technology can be attained by studying and earning certifications.

Online study tools like CompTIA's CertMaster help students study and pass their certification exams. To appeal to young people and the ways they learn best, CertMaster adapts video-game techniques to make the lessons stick. The interactive app keeps track of the questions that seem to cause hesitation and adjusts the lesson to focus on more challenging areas. Students learn from wrong answers and begin to understand their trouble areas, which boosts confidence and releases endorphins, motivating students to keep working.

In major cities, programs like Cities of Learning promote technology, giving kids a place to explore and expand their interests while teaching them soft skills like communication, management and leadership — important personal skills that can help a young technology professional land a job.

Look for city-wide programs for kids and recent high school graduates in Atlanta, Baltimore, Boston, Chicago, Washington, D.C., New York, Minneapolis, Dallas, San Francisco, Seattle and Pittsburgh. Our Creating IT Futures staff members travel the country and see lots of innovative programs in towns big and small. If you don't see a program in your area featured in this book, rest assured that there's likely something nearby.

Year Up helps urban young adults gain the skills and experience they need to join the information technology industry, empowering them to reach their potential through professional careers and higher education. They offer education, training and career placement.

Photo from Vocademy

Makerspaces are an evolution of the craftsman and artisan enclaves that naturally develop in society.

Genesys Works is a nonprofit social enterprise that enables disadvantaged high school students to succeed through meaningful work experience. Students spend eight high octane weeks in an intensive IT training program and then work at a client company for a hands-on corporate tech experience.

IT-Ready works with nonprofits around the country to teach people the technical skills needed for IT, plus the soft skills employers seek in job candidates. Creating IT Futures founded IT-Ready to help people gain real-world experience so that they can launch their tech careers.

Similarly, a partner of Creating IT Futures, Per Scholas, offers accelerated tech support classes plus quality assurance, networking and cybersecurity classes. The nonprofit is based in New York City, with classes there and in Atlanta, Cincinnati, Columbus, Dallas and Washington, D.C.

Makerspaces Make Time for Fun and Exploration

Before diving into a class, your child might want to explore makerspaces and hackerspaces that encourage construction, creation and group

I'M A TECHNOLOGIST, TOO

Dale Burkett
Chief of Staff, VP & GM Office Software
Defined Infrastructure

DALE BURKETT WAS AN UNLIKELY CANDIDATE for a tech career. He grew up in Trinidad, a Caribbean country where, in the 1970s and 1980s, computers were rare.

Burkett convinced his father that computers would teach him a lot of things, and talked his father into buying one. "Dad had the foresight to make that investment in my future," he said. When his family immigrated to Brooklyn, Burkett was delighted to find computers in his school. In high school, he focused on learning everything he could about the machines.

Thinking a degree would help him learn even more about computers, Burkett enrolled in college at City College of New York for electrical engineering. Surprisingly, he found himself losing interest in classes. So he took some time off to work for Macy's in the store's electronics department.

"I needed a new start," he said, and he transferred to North Carolina State University in Raleigh to study mechanical engineering. That helped him understand the cooling, components and measurements of a circuit board. Even more important, he fell in love with the problem-solving nature of engineering.

"The engineer is no longer the guy with the pocket protector. It's someone who sees a need and develops something to meet that need," he said. "Just having that inquisitive nature and the methodology to figure out a solution is important."

collaboration, and offer kids and teens the freedom to experiment with the technology they like best.

In a typical makerspace, you might see a crowd in the corner playing a piano. Not your typical piano, though. This one has only five keys, which are all made from cucumbers. Kids will be shaping Play-Doh into left/right and up/down buttons, jamming in cords and firing up a circuit board to play a replica game of Pac-Man. You'll hear the hum of activity as plastic bottles churn water for a sustainable tilapia tank, and you'll see 3-D printers popping out customized key rings and toys.

As 3-D printers, laser cutters and other digital prototyping tools gain power and come down in price, community makerspaces grow in popularity. Alex Bandar, PhD, called it the "democratization of opportunity."

"Like computers over the last 30 years, these tools have become cheaper, smaller and yet paradoxically more powerful and more approachable," said Bandar, who, in 2008, started the two-floor, 60,000-square-foot Columbus Idea Foundry in Ohio as a resource for schools that didn't have wood, machine or metal shops.

Similarly, Vocademy is a 15,000-square-foot facility in Riverside, California, acting as a hybrid between shop class and trade school. "We pride ourselves on being the education-focused makerspace," said founder Gene Sherman.

Makerspaces can be housed anywhere, from mall storefronts to community centers and even people's backyards. A lot of kids are hands-on learners, and if you want to get them into technology right away, one of the best ways to do that is to get them involved in a makerspace.

"Makerspaces have to be organic, they cannot be forced or mandated," said Sherman. Each makerspace is unique, and the projects done within the group reflect the tools, resources and interests of its members.

It's challenging to convince parents that hands-on education can benefit all students, not just those who struggle with academics, Sherman said. "That stereotype judges people on how intelligent they *are* versus *how are they* intelligent," Sherman said. "It's such a big difference."

Hackerspaces are different from makerspaces, but not by much. Their members focus on electronics, web development and information security, and sometimes members get together to hack away on a joint software project.

Photo from REC Foundation

Robotics is a good introduction to technology because it's self-paced, from beginner to competition level.

Robots Engage Students

Ten years ago, Jackie Moore was on the hunt for an engaging educational solution for her son. He was 9 at the time and what she called "a different kind of learner." He was smart, curious and creative, but didn't respond to the way schools tried to teach him.

"If he wasn't interested, he just didn't pay attention. He'd glaze right over," she said.

Searching for a solution, she started Chicago Knights, a FIRST robotics team that gave her son, her daughters and their friends the opportunity to work with others to solve problems and compete in FIRST's national challenges using robots. In 2011, she founded LevelUP IRL, a teen focused makerspace that provides the opportunity to work on additional kinetic, interactive and intelligent technology projects. Moore is a mother of four who had already found enough opportunity in technology to build a career for herself but wanted to provide those opportunities to others. She also opened the world of creation and technology to hundreds of neighborhood families through several FIRST robotics teams.

"What I've learned early and what has been confirmed over the years is that technology is the great equalizer," said Moore, who worked in information technology for more than 25 years. Technology let her be judged by her work and not her status as a young, black female. In the robotics teams, students are not judged by their age or ability, but rather on what

I'M A TECHNOLOGIST, TOO

Brad Flora
Entrepreneur, Tech Angel Investor
Marin Software

BRAD FLORA WORKED as a journalist and college admissions officer before finding his niche in information technology.

As an entrepreneur looking to run his own business, he turned to online advertising, and found a way to help companies buy it more efficiently. He used the skills he built up in college admissions to prepare investor pitches and successfully launched PerfectAudience.com. In 2014, a San Francisco software company bought his business, and he stayed on as senior director of product management.

For those about to rock the tech world with their new ideas, Flora recommends building up expertise and working with the smartest people you can find.

they create and how they work with others. The teams are heavy on collaboration, and students lead whenever possible.

"When they make something and see that it works, there's a real sense of achievement," Moore said. "Some students don't get that in other places, but they get it here, and no one can take that away from them."

Robotics is a popular hobby in makerspaces. Introductory kits get kids going at a manageable speed and the projects grow more challenging along the way.

"Everyone approaches robotics with common sense, in an intuitive way, using trial and error," said Armando Diegoperez, of VEX Robotics Design System, which makes a set of snap-to-gether robot-building kits for beginners, as well as competi-tion-grade parts for advanced builders.

Simple machine learning is based on common sense and intuitive curiosity. When a kid stacks a block on a wheel set and says *vroom vroom*, he's playing and creating. Those same repre-sentational abilities translate to robotics. Dynamic learning starts when kids figure out what the parts actually do, and then ar-range them according to a plan. It's called "systematizing the procedures" in robotics terms. Kids naturally start learning the processes required to make things work.

> "I don't think there's a right or wrong path — I think there's a path for you."
>
> —Former high school IT teacher Eric Berngen

Robotics also lends itself to a number of areas of interaction: design, structure, motion, energy, sensors, control, logic and programming. "Each involves differentiated knowledge and will be as strong as the interest of each student," Diegoperez said.

Like other technology exercises, robotics lets kids dabble in different ac-tivities, excel where they feel comfortable and collaborate with others. Robotics tournaments offer even more lessons in specialized divisions of labor and take students through the ups and downs of competition.

'There's a Path for You'

There are a lot of ways to get your child involved in technology, and no route is better than another.

"I'm working on my third degree since high school, and college did wonders for me," said former IT teacher Eric Berngen. "My sister, on the other hand, has got a truckload of certifications and she works for J.P. Morgan Chase, making six figures plus," he said. "I don't think there's a right or wrong path — I think there's a path for you."

THE TAKEAWAY

Teenagers can learn technology skills through classes, clubs and online research. A skills-based certification like CompTIA A+ can be an important first step toward a career in technology.

Where the Jobs Are

Technology Is Essential to Business

TODAY'S TECHNOLOGY PROFESSIONALS hold leading roles in software development, mobile technologies, cybersecurity and big data. They consider the customer and use their communication skills to find creative solutions to the customers' problems. People who understand technology have a seat at the boardroom table, too, and help determine the future of their organizations.

"Information technology does not mean one thing anymore," said Angelo Simao, whose firm matches companies with technology professionals to work on all sorts of projects. "IT is going to touch every industry."

Technology Makes Sports More Interactive

I love sports. I use a bunch of different apps to check on my favorite teams as I travel, and I have a whole routine to help me follow the latest scouting reports for Duke University's basketball recruits.

Two Distinct Components of the Tech Workforce

Technology jobs are available in and outside of the IT industry, with about half the technical jobs outside of IT industry employers.

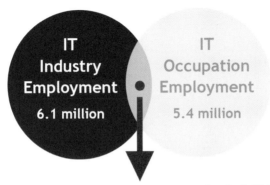

An estimated 6.1 million workers were employed in the U.S. information technology industry in 2017. This includes technical and non-technical positions in employer firms and non-employer firms.

Within the IT industry, there are many IT occupations and IT workers

An estimated 5.4 million workers were employed in core IT occupations, across the full spectrum of U.S. industry sectors and the government sector in 2017. This figure includes non-employers, such as the self-employed and sole proprietors.

Source: Bureau of Labor Statistics, EMSI and CompTIA

Sports teams around the nation harness the power of technology to improve their teams and bring more fans to the games. While left-handed relief pitchers and right-handed power hitters will always be eyed by general managers in Major League Baseball, a search of another sort is underway at MLB Advanced Media, the interactive media and internet company of our national pastime.

Crowned by CBS News as "one of the tech world's top players," MLB Advanced Media is a digital behemoth, delivering an estimated $110 million annually to each of MLB's 30 teams. The full-service solutions provider delivers digital experiences and distributes content for web, mobile applications and connected devices while integrating live and on-demand multimedia. In late 2016, MLB Advanced Media announced a $300 million deal to partner with Riot Games to stream the popular e-sport game League of Legends. Clearly, they are about more than just baseball.

The use of technology in athletics has made a great impact on the way many sports are played.

Visit their website and you'll find job openings for data engineers, information security compliance architects, database engineers, and mobile and responsive web app developers — dozens of technology jobs ripe for the picking.

A lot of those jobs are entry-level, but even entry-level technology jobs can be interesting, particularly when it comes to sports. Robert Blanchard hires a lot of first-timers for his team, which handles all the technology-related problems for Aspen Skiing Co., a four-mountain chain of destination resorts in the remote Rocky Mountains. "Everything on our mountain is computerized," he said.

The team uses software to track which trails were groomed overnight plus how much snow fell and its consistency. Additional software communicates with the trail grooming machines, called Snowcats, to track mileage, GPS information, acres per hour, gas and other usage data. Another program runs the snowmaking guns.

"Somebody can sit at sort of a control desk and tell a certain valve to turn on or off, how much water to pump to a certain location or how much air to pump," Blanchard said. Without technology professionals to make those critical calculations, the lines can freeze and explode.

Running the helpdesk for a destination ski resort isn't what most people think of when it comes to tech careers, but this busy group of outdoorsmen and women enjoy their indoor-outdoor lifestyle.

"When things slow down," Blanchard said. "I can send two or three people out skiing for an hour or two."

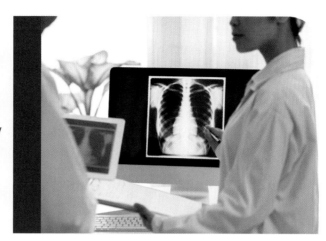

Doctors and nurses rely on technologists to track data, keep records secure and stay current with life-saving tools.

Doctors Rely on Technology

When a cardiologist's computer system goes down, it's a company like Amy Kardel's Clever Ducks that comes to the rescue. "If one of our medical practice groups can't access a record, can't print, or just needs some technical support, they would call us," she said.

Doctors rely on technology for medical management and monitoring, displaying X-ray and MRI results, accessing electronic health records (EHR) and helping patients with insurance claims.

"We help them with the software and hardware to do all that," said Kardel, whose technical team includes people who have earned CompTIA A+, Network+ and Security+ certifications.

The U.S. healthcare system is becoming more digital and more mobile, driven in large part by changes in healthcare policies. Working with technicians helps physicians alter their perceptions about technology.

Once they see how remote health monitoring and telemedicine can extend and enhance the care they provide to patients, they're open to expanding digital and electronic technologies to improve care, streamline administrative processes and lower costs.

Healthcare is alive with hybrid jobs that mix some degree of healthcare knowledge with technology expertise. Job growth is expected in clinical application support, information technology management, financial application support, security, project management, clinical informatics, and system design and implementation.

I'M A TECHNOLOGIST, TOO

Kelly Stone
Director, Social Media
CompTIA

SOCIAL MEDIA IS an emerging field, where it's easy to experiment without a lot of risk. Use it well, and you can make big things happen — like the social media campaign Kelly Stone ran that landed on John Oliver's Last Week Tonight and helped a school raise $40,000 for scholarships.

"Because it's a nimble and emerging technology, you have the ability to alter course quickly, and that's very empowering in communications and in creativity," she said.

It's easy to measure your success in social media. "You can see clearly how you're helping a company reach their bottom line goals," she said.

Thanks to her company's flexible work-from-home option, she can train for triathlons and keep up her active lifestyle blog, where she uses her skills to support her personal interests. "On some days, I get up super early, work for a bit, ride my bike, work for a couple more hours and run again in the afternoon. It's nice to have that freedom and that ability."

For students looking to get into technology, Stone recommends good communication skills.

"Our studies have shown it's the soft skills that set you apart. Learn social graces, learn networking with people, but realize that your biggest job in life is to solve problems and make your boss look good," she said. "The more you can do that, the further you can go."

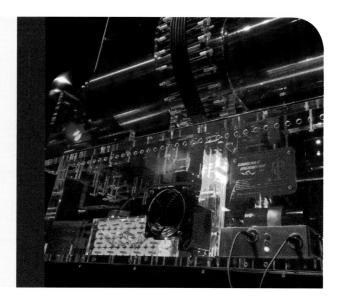

Photo by Eric Goodchild

Tinkering can turn into a whole career. Eric Goodchild took his love for Tesla coils and turned it into an education and entertainment business.

"Everyone needs a lawyer, a doctor and an IT pro," Kardel said. "Even the smallest towns in America need a lot of technology help."

Technology Drives Automotive Innovation

In May 2015, German Mercedes-Benz maker Daimler announced a partnership with Qualcomm to explore wireless recharging innovations for mobile phones and electric vehicles. Imagine: An electric car you could juice up automatically, with no fill station or plug required.

In January 2017, Ford Motor Company and Amazon announced a collaborative program integrating Alexa, a digital assistant operated by voice command, into Ford vehicles. The Alexa integration — the most comprehensive ever in a vehicle — allows Ford owners to play and resume audiobooks, order items on Amazon, search for and transfer local destinations to the in-car navigation system, and more. From home, Ford vehicle owners can remote start, lock or unlock doors and get vehicle information using voice commands.

"We believe voice is the future, and this is particularly true in cars. The ability to use your voice to control your smart home, access entertainment, manage to-do lists and more makes for an extraordinary driving experience," said Steve Rabuchin, vice president of Amazon Alexa, in a news release from CES 2017, one of the biggest technology expos in the world.[23]

General Motors soon will test new Cisco Systems technology that could allow cars to share radio communication bands with roadside wi-fi devices. Talking cars, they call them. The company's also working hard to integrate tablets, touchscreens and mobile technology into its vehicles, creating more demand for technology professionals in the auto industry.

Innovative ideas like these keep us tuned keenly to advances in the automotive industry. Progress also means analytics experts, web programmers and sustainability integration pros are increasingly in demand in the automotive sector.

"Succeeding in the technology industry isn't any different from any other industry," said Mary Ellen Grom, who uses technology to power marketing at the fiber optics company AFL. "Define what it is you want to pursue and imagine a place or a role for yourself."

Grom's son wants to work for a company that manufactures high-end cars like Maseratis and Lamborghinis. She encourages him to explore robotics and other technologies used on the manufacturing line. "Kids can apply technology to whatever career they pursue," Grom said.

Technology Boosts an Artist's Creativity

Technology is a great place for creative people, too. Eric Goodchild started Plasma Phonic Inc. as a hobby and now builds museum exhibits and visual shows founded on years of tinkering with Tesla coils and other technology. His mom's career was inspirational to his work. Ellen Lichtwardt worked with George Lucas and Steven Spielberg during the golden age of Lucas' production company, Industrial Light and Magic.

She was part of the original team that produced special effects for *Return of the Jedi*, *Indiana Jones* and *ET*. "That's when the technical side started coming on my radar," she said. "George Lucas was very hands on, walking around the studio and saying things like, 'We have to produce this kind of an effect and it's never been done before. How are we going to do it?' Everyone was given free rein to try to come up with the answer."

She worked on practical effects like puppets, robotics and elaborate miniatures to bring life to films like *Back to the Future*. Directors Steven

23. News release: January 4, 2017; Ford Motor Company MediaCenter.
  bit.ly/FordplusAlexaNews

I'M A TECHNOLOGIST, TOO

Cassandra Anderson
Director of Sales Enablement
Nextiva

CASSANDRA ANDERSON STUMBLED into the technology industry while working in an adolescent drug rehab center that needed an upgrade to its phone and computer systems. "In working with the local phone installer, I realized the technology fascinated me," she said.

She impressed the company with her questions and people skills, and they asked her to come on board as a customer trainer. "I made the switch and after 18 years — and so many wonderful positions in the technology industry — I have never looked back," she said.

The industry's constant evolution is what got her. "There are always new products and concepts to learn and share. I have the opportunity to help businesses improve and to make a difference," she said.

She encourages women to look at technology as not just technical, but as a creative way to change the world. "We can make change," she said. "One solution at a time."

Spielberg and Robert Zemeckis came in to work with Lucas' artistic and technology teams.

"Eventually we started getting computerized cameras, and I started to see the crossover of digital into the traditional, hands-on way of doing

Farmers are using technology tools to observe, measure and respond to variability in their crops.

things," she said. She urged animator friends to jump on the computer and start learning design programs like Adobe Photoshop and Illustrator to enhance their skills — a message she's been sharing for 30 years.

"With creativity, you have to really experience it. In music, for example, you can compose songs with digital software, but it's going to be even better if you know what it sounds like to have piano keys or strings under your fingers," Lichtwardt said. "You need to really experience with all of yourself the creative process and then use this fantastic technology as a tool to take it beyond the original work."

Technology Helps Feed the World

Technology has even worked its way into the cornfields of Iowa, thanks to a growing precision technology industry that is helping farmers apply technology to their fields for better efficiency. "There's a whole techno-farming revolution happening," said Arlin Sorensen, founder of HTS Ag.

Tools used in precision agriculture help farmers maximize the yield. GPS tracking, for example, plants seeds within a fraction of an inch of the plan, while sensors keep tabs on tractors, combines and planters to optimize fuel consumption and maximize machinery output.

"These units can steer things perfectly, and you overlay that with technology and thousands of acres of corn and soybeans — that makes a difference," Sorensen said.

Mapping the IT Jobs Landscape

The top 25 states for IT occupations account for 88 percent of total IT jobs.

1 California
2 Texas
3 New York
4 Florida
5 Virginia
6 Illinois
7 Pennsylvania
8 Washington
9 New Jersey
10 Massachusetts
11 Georgia
12 Ohio
13 North Carolina
14 Maryland   20 Wisconsin
15 Michigan   21 Indiana
16 Colorado   22 Oregon
17 Minnesota   23 Tennessee
18 Arizona   24 Connecticut
19 Missouri   25 Utah

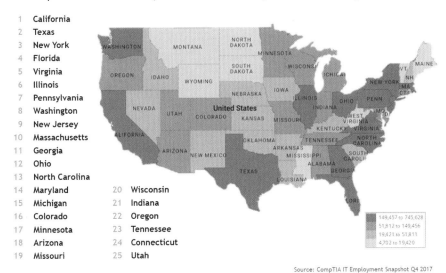

149,457 to 745,628
51,812 to 149,456
19,421 to 51,811
4,702 to 19,420

Source: CompTIA IT Employment Snapshot Q4 2017

Technology helps monitor storage, too, making sure the crop is at the right temperature, with the right moisture level. "Through remote monitoring and management, I can look at my computer and see the exact humidity, temperature and moisture, which allows the system to automatically kick on the fans or the propane so that when the grain is delivered to market, the crop will be at its fullest value," he said.

Farmers also use drones in the fields to monitor growing conditions and make real-time adjustments to key growing challenges like weed pressure, insects or fungus. Technology is used to test and monitor the soil. Technology is a boon to the challenging industry of farming, which relies on things one can't control, like weather and market prices.

"Farming is a bigger gamble than going to Vegas, where at least you get to pick your game," Sorensen said. Precision technology can't solve a two-month drought, but at least farmers can be far more proactive than reactive in many areas of production agriculture. "It certainly helps when they have productivity tools that are technologically driven."

Technologists working in finance ease payment processes, reduce fraud and save users money.

Technology Makes Finance More Profitable

Finance technology, sometimes called fintech, uses software to help people manage their money. It can be simple, like an app that helps you keep a budget, or complex, like web-based trading grounded in analytical algorithms. In our work, we deal in budgets, payroll and finances all the time, and technology helps us make sense of what's coming and going. Whether they're helping individuals or major corporations, the financial services industry is always looking for ways to cut costs, comply with changing regulations and stay competitive. Because the industry is always innovating, people are willing to invest: By 2021, IT spending will reach $2.7 trillion, with the largest contributions coming from consumers, banks, manufacturers, and telecommunications providers, according to a worldwide technology spending forecast by IDC. IT budgets in the financial services sector will jump more than 5 percent. [24]

Cloud computing is leading these emerging technologies, giving companies the tools to improve efficiencies and stay competitive. Cybersecurity is getting attention, too, thanks to headlines warning of large-scale data breaches.

Financial technology is an enterprising field to get involved in, recom-

24. International Data Corporation (IDC) Worldwide Semi-Annual IT Spending Guide: Industry and Company Size, July 2017
bit.ly/IDC-IT-Spending-Guide-2018

I'M A TECHNOLOGIST, TOO

Mario Cadet
Support Service Manager
ASI System Integration

IT'S HARD TO PREDICT how each day will go for Mario Cadet. A frantic email can reprioritize his whole day, but it's that kind of variety he likes — the kind that keeps the day moving fast. "You never stop learning in IT," he said.

Cadet started as a technician, was promoted to lead technician and worked his way up to supervisor. How far you go in the industry depends on you. "The sky's the limit," he said.

Now he's a service delivery manager with a daily schedule that involves managing people, interacting with clients and solving problems. "It's very rewarding," he said. "I take seriously the position I have, and I really love it a lot."

mended for those who are unafraid to explore unchartered waters.

Technology professionals are in the best position to explore new solutions, and industries are finally catching on to that. Healthcare, education, government, finance, entertainment, sports — everyone's hungry for tech workers who think strategically, can communicate effectively, have strong business fundamentals and are creative in identifying how to use technology to make a business operate more efficiently and profitably.

"Everything has a technology spin to it," Simao said. "It's not just coding or fixing the hardware. In everything — law, entertainment, fashion, everything — there's a lot of IT."

Technology Is a Mindset, Not a Job Title

If you've watched *24*, *Person of Interest*, *Scandal* or many other recent TV shows and movies, you're familiar with pop culture's latest version of a computer whiz and hacker. Often quirky, probably snarky. These characters march to the beat of their own drum, and they make a computer do things faster and more graphically elaborate than anyone could in the real world.

I spoke to a movie producer last year who said the biggest problem with portraying tech jobs on screen is that they just aren't cinematic. Audiences wouldn't want to see how long it really takes to hack a computer or find malware.

As an aside, if you want to see a solid depiction of cybersecurity and hacking, watch *Mr. Robot*. The storyline might be a bit unsettling to some, but the tech action is dead on.

We may enjoy watching many of those hacker characters, but they're a bit more offbeat than the folks we know in tech. People working in information technology are just like people you know, and most got into the industry through straightforward career choices, not because they wanted to hack the Pentagon.

Here's a more realistic version of a tech professional: Fashion designer Alyssa Frame, who works in Milwaukee, Wisconsin, is clever, a great problem solver, and does her job well without a stitch of ill-fitting clothing or thick glasses.

"I've always loved fashion and started integrating technology into my designs very early on," she said. "I work with programs like Illustrator to create my designs, send them to factories all over the world and have real products come back to me."

She uses radio frequency identification tags and specialized tracking software to keep tabs on thousands of dresses, tops and accessories, all in real time.

"Retail is the end-result of months — sometimes years — of planning, from the design to the buying to the manufacturing," she said.

Technology helps make those processes more efficient and shorten that lead time. While the transfer, parsing and exchange of huge data files might not inspire the glamour of New York Fashion Week, information

I'M A TECHNOLOGIST, TOO

John Holst
Senior Manager, Content & Design
CompTIA

THE DIVERSITY OF the people and their careers surprised John Holst when he got into the technology industry. "I thought IT would be more like, alone, on a computer by yourself," said Holst. "I realize now it's a lot more collaborative than I thought it would be."

Holst works with a variety of people to build websites and manage all the content produced by his company. The most challenging part of his job is making sure that artists, designers, coders, marketers and project managers are all on the same page.

"The most rewarding part of the job is when we launch a piece of content or site and it launches well," he said.

As the industry grows, more companies will need people to manage content and fix websites. That means job security for someone with people skills and a handful of marketable tech skills. "You're always going to need someone to manage content, or fix websites," he said. "I think it's always going to be a career that has stability and something I can rely on in my life going forward."

technologists are using these tools to get you into your favorite new dress much faster than before.

"The real-time inventory we can track with radio-frequency identification, or RFID, means hassle-free pick-up in the store," Frame said.

I'M A TECHNOLOGIST, TOO

Alyissa Dzaugis
Product Manager
Robin Powered

AFTER EARNING HER Masters of Fine Arts degree from the University of Wisconsin, Alyissa Dzaugis found a job working for Pearson, an educational publishing company that also has a hand in technology.

That experience opened her up to the world of tech startups, where her background in art and film came in surprisingly handy. The humanities taught her to think creatively, react quickly and work well on a team — crucial skills for the startup world. Today she's a product manager for a tech startup called Robin Powered, a scheduling platform for offices.

"Marrying technology and the humanities is really powerful. It helps you see problems in new ways," Dzaugis said.

RFID uses electromagnetic fields to identify and track tags attached to objects.

"You know your order will be there, because we're analyzing our sales data to make sure all of our stores are stocked with the right merchandise," said Frame.

Technology also is helping fast-fashion edge into the apparel market. Flash sites that advertise cute earrings at a huge discount during pop-up sales require the smart use of technology tools.

"I didn't get into fashion to be a technologist, but these days it's crazy to think about how companies tracked merchandise without the help of technology," Frame said.

Advocating for Your Child

"Opportunities to work with technology pop up everywhere, if you're curious and motivated," said Andrea Rios McMillian, a colleague of mine at Creating IT Futures who spends a lot of time helping parents explain the benefits of technology to their children.

"Advocating for your kid's future as a technologist is all about connecting the dots between their strengths and interests and the millions of ways technology is relevant to every business in every industry across the country and around the world," said McMillian, a mother of three boys. "Yes, the possibilities are that grandiose."

McMillian has worked with Chicago's Early College STEM Schools, which help high school students work toward diplomas, associate's degrees and IT industry certifications while gaining industry mentorship and experience.

With funding from the Chicagoland Workforce Funder Alliance, the schools collaborate with employers to connect them with students for internships, mentoring, school visits, classroom projects and speaking opportunities.

When you're advocating for a future in technology, McMillian believes, you're not trying to sell an isolated, boring existence where your kid's eyes are glued to a screen. Technology's being used in farming, fashion, finance and film — any field where your child has an interest.

"Like any discussion about your child's future, advocating for technology is about your relationship," McMillian said. "It's about trust, about working shoulder to shoulder with your kid."

THE TAKEAWAY

Technology plays a role in millions of ways in thousands of businesses. Jobs using technology are exciting, diverse and creative — from grooming ski slopes to making movies. And jobs in technology are plentiful and in demand. Technology offers opportunities for everyone.

Why We Rally for the T in STEM

Opportunities for Every Teen

NOW YOU'VE SEEN what a technology career could look like for your child. You've met people doing interesting work and collaborating happily with people they respect. Information technology careers offer enormous possibilities, and we hope we've piqued your excitement enough that you will want to explore it for your kids and maybe even yourself.

Parents are the best at spotting their kids' talents and knowing their personality traits, and your child depends on you to help them find the way. Think your kids aren't listening? From their earliest years, the place kids hear the most stories is at home. Parents and other family members share their experiences in living and working with their children to teach, guide and reassure them that they, too, can learn and grow.

"By virtue of time, a child's understanding of the world is shallow compared to that of an adult," said textbook author and college instructor Jill West. She also is a mother of four.

"Kids have big gaps in their knowledge that they depend on us to help them fill. And one of the things they learn from us is how to learn," West said. "Because no one — including teachers and counselors — knows them better than you do."

I'M A TECHNOLOGIST, TOO

Melissa Lopez
Manager, Command Center
ASI System Integration

THE WAY MELISSA LOPEZ SEES IT, the IT industry truly is an equal opportunity employer.

"I definitely believe women can succeed just as much as men in IT," said Lopez, command center manager for ASI System Integration. "The female technicians that work here — the field technicians, the system engineers — are some of our best people."

In her role at ASI System Integration, Lopez ensures that customers get the technical support they need.

"The computer is used for so many things — paying bills, running businesses — so when the computer is down, making sure that it is running again is my main concern," she said.

And the IT industry definitely represents opportunity for people who enjoy working with others.

"People skills are important," she said. "Even when you don't know exactly what to do, having people skills and a proper dialogue with the customer gives you the opportunity to figure it out or time to look it up."

For women who are motivated, the IT industry has no glass ceiling, Lopez said.

"The more you learn, the more you're worth," she said. "Technology is a great field to be in because it's in everything, and it's growing every day. This is a technology world."

As a parent, you don't have to be an expert on technology careers to spot and support the abilities of your child. The knowledge kids crave from parents is not technical.

"What kids need are real-life, real-world examples of living and working," she said. "We don't have to know how all the tech in their lives works to help them fill gaps in their understanding. We just have to help them question their understanding and challenge them to set high personal standards of knowledge."

"You don't have to have all the answers," West continued. "Just ask good questions. You know more than you realize."

In Creating IT Futures' *Teen Views on Tech Careers* study, we asked teens who they rely on most to talk about their future careers. The most frequent answer was "parents and guardians." At 68 percent, that answer was given more than two times more often than "teachers" (28 percent) and "school counselors" (25 percent).[25]

If anyone can spot technology promise in your child, it's you. Share with them everything you've read so far: Technology is about solving problems, creating solutions, learning from failure, helping people and discovering opportunity. It's important that students recognize the characteristics of a technology professional and can identify some of those traits within themselves.

Technology will continue to advance, and we need thoughtful, empathetic and talented people to be a part of the industry's growth. Let your children know, let their friends know and let the world know that information technology is a place for everyone.

Whether she wants to travel the world or stay in the neighborhood, there's a place in technology for your daughter. Same for your son. Let them experience the pride in solving a difficult problem, or being the essential ingredient to a successful team.

Throughout the book, we talked to artists and engineers, communicators and designers, hackers and makers, moms and dads. They all told us the same thing: Couple technology with any career interest and your teen will have a chance to make something, do something and be something.

25. Creating IT Futures *Teen Views on Tech Careers Survey, February 2015.*
   www.creatingitfutures.org/researching-solutions/teen-views-on-tech-careers

FACT: Technology is about logic, not math.

People working in technology break problems into pieces and examine the parts to find the connections between them that may be causing complications or creating obstacles. In doing so, they're practicing a basic intellectual skill: logic.

Yes, logic sometimes is communicated through mathematics. But equations are just one way of expressing logical thinking. There are dozens of other ways to apply logic. Working with puzzles is essentially working with logic. Playing video games involves logic. Building models or Lego sets are logical exercises. For that matter, even following recipes or product manuals offers valuable practice in the type of problem solving we do in technology.

In this book, you've seen dozens of ways educators and business people — many of them parents — use logic to apply technology to meet an objective and succeed. And none of those examples involved solving complicated math equations.

FACT: Technology is about hands-on solutions.

People working in technology arrange pieces of processes and parts of hardware and software into solutions. In doing so, they're behaving like engineers, who take a hands-on approach to building things.

The best engineers enjoy exploring pieces and parts, and tinkering with the different ways they can be put together and still function successfully. Whether or not your kid wants an engineering degree, the spirit of an engineer enables a future as a technology professional.

FACT: Technology is about learning from failure.

People working in technology investigate cause and effect by trial and error. In doing so, they learn as much from failure as they do from success. Failure can reveal logical relationships more quickly than success, a statement that more or less sums up the life of a scientist.

Our point here is similar to our point about math: Whether or not your kid gets good grades in science, time spent experimenting is valuable practice for a future as a technology professional.

FACT: Technology is about helping people.

Results from Creating IT Futures' *Teen Views on Tech Careers* study showed us teens want to help their families and contribute to making situations and circumstances better for everyone involved. Similar research demonstrates likeminded motivations among aspiring scientists and engineers. While the T in STEM is different in many ways than science, engineering and math, it's similar in terms of intent and benefit.

So, just as people proficient in science, engineering and mathematics do a lot to help our society, technologists do, too. Think of all the people you met in this book, all the challenges they help others overcome, all the problems they solve for businesses and all the industries they keep moving forward. It's all about making things work better, not just working with cool stuff. And making things better is really all about finding ways to help people.

FACT: Technology is about discovering opportunity.

There are hundreds of ways your child could end up a technologist, and the opportunities continue to grow as new technologies hit the market. Ten years ago we couldn't have imagined how many people would be needed to create and update mobile applications. Who would have thought that IT pros would become the next mechanics as automated vehicles are poised to enter our everyday lives. Even doctors are becoming technologists as they work with health wearables and remote monitoring systems to benefit their patients.

Jobs in tech are plentiful and in demand. Technology offers career opportunities for everyone, and it's why we rally for the T in STEM.

THANK YOU

THIS BOOK WAS MADE POSSIBLE by the efforts of so many people. It has gone through several rewrites, many edits and an update thanks to the great work of R.C. Dirkes, Lisa Fasold, Michelle Lange and Todd Thibodeaux. We wouldn't have even thought about a guide for parents without a terrific brainstorming session with the Creating IT Futures board of directors. And we wouldn't have known where to start without the technology community providing their insights and sharing their stories. Thank you to everyone.

I also want to thank Amy Carrado, Celine Dirkes, David Dritsas, Robert Fine, Dan Green, Melissa Hart, Eric Larson, Tom Liszka, Stacy Litwin, Jamie Marturano, Jeff O'Heir, and Steven Ostrowski for their help putting this all together.